アンチテーゼ

Antithesis

Haiku

Jacob Kobina Ayiah Mensah

Acknowledgments

Thank you to the following journals and anthologies for first publishing these haiku, most in earlier forms:

Modern Haiku (volume 49.3 Autumn 2018, under the Spotlight): "in some cases", "opening the funeral", "old pages", "cold air leans", "raindrop collapsing", "full moonlit", "the stone's indifference", "rough draft", "(st", " | within | ", "women out there", "a row of newly", "experience of the stones", "the rain nearly", "BITINGGGGGGG", "winter stillness", "candlelight around", and "winter night".

World Haiku (anthology, 2010 # 6): "from light years", "the tallest waterfall", and "between my hands".

World Haiku (anthology, 2011 # 7): "Ashanti doll", "two rocks", and "Ljubljana veal cutlet".

World Haiku (anthology, 2013 # 9): "to the north", "my life story", and "banana republic".

World Haiku (anthology, 2015 # 11): "an image", "under", and "something good".

World Haiku (anthology, 2016 # 12): "around secant", "Congo mathematics", and "domain of a shadow".

World haiku (anthology, 2018 # 14): "leaving a single footprint", "Rainbow", and "noontide".

NOON journal of the short poem (ISSUE 15, August 2015): "digging through".

NOON journal of the short poem (ISSUE 13, March 2017): "deep silence", and "smoke".

failed haiku (Volume 2, Issue 20): "a level access", "behind mirrors", "whirlwind", and "starry night".

Otata (14, February 2017): "a feather falls", "thunder rolling", "suddenly a corner", "this foreign area", "stillness has fallen", "i am hosting", "rain bubbles", "spring to", "distance nears", "drinking", "a star burning", and "that wind like".

The Mamba (March 2017): "partially clouds"

Contents

Responsible blue for many of the most significant innovations: introduction
Author's note
Haiku

Responsible blue for many of the most significant innovations: introduction

Haiku has grown beyond its size and now undergoing major changings. Japan cannot say it owns haiku completely as England cannot say it owns English language. Like any language, every creator of haiku owns it. This is the *responsible blue*. The more haiku creator owns haiku the more he looks for the most significant innovations that will release the practice from nugget. This is why I like haiku that engage with the influx of people, matter and imagery that combine at any level, or that is sought to widen the controversy, designating as a path for certification, or both. Differences of opinion prevail, however, as to whether such practices are desirable, I have no institution to guarantee this individual endorsement. We cannot forget that we pay for every composition of the audience for any progress. This is where I am trying to work from and express a small number of common underlying cultural themes. To those who espouse the conception of culture will reproduce tension and find this field the adopted standard. However, I cannot leave these questions of aftermath behind any human institution. Why art? Why imagination and experience? Why beauty and aesthetics? Why truth and falsehood? We look for answers with anomalous normality. Beyond these, I find other considerations that weight heavily in accrediting judgments. Does one have to limit himself to objects and events that are found in his locality or explore the world as he travels? Who determines the subjects and themes for an artist? Opening oneself to different rooms is a kind of reasoning. The ascent of haiku compositions appearing in publications may be explained by a number of different factors. The details go far beyond what I can say here. The loosely bounded cultures that exert no artistic control may account for that. Artists have to paint with words, using kitchen knife to scratch the surface of the canvas for additional light, or sculpting words. Artists have to do what they want to do. Haiku offers them a large variety of possibilities for this labour. I am looking at the visual language of texture and light and through the intensely atmospheric natural structures seen in the picture. We are using a highly efficient process of communication. Quite the opposite is nearer the truth. Haiku is the discipline, posing questions about the nature of human activity — in the past, in the present and in the future. The more the past, the more we make the present, and the more the present the more we make the future, and more we make the future the more we make haiku. Despite the demographics and the massive readings available we need to do more workings to understand the art of haiku than still relying heavily on rules of thumb.

In this collection, that explores the issues including social interaction, consumption, waste and the contradictions that form the dynamics of everyday life, I am trying to expand the kind of haiku I have called *antitheses* and I believe that any time we create haiku, we define more haiku. Though this may lead to the formulation and I do not substantiate this claim. However, I am trying to avoid all this. I am happy that I am fascinating with found imagery from debris, history and the street. This is the formulaic logic of haiku, having an appearance that is antipathetic to hard flash and I welcome discussions and debates on this kind. Thus, in painting and collaging, I vary in format and cater for different levels in words and signs or symbols.

Jacob Kobina Ayiah Mensah

Author's note

Haiku appearing in another language is a version and not translation. However, where haiku in different languages are the same is just unfortunate, leading to many questions. Every language has its body and spirit in all developed broadcasting systems and I allow the art to have its mould there as a complete whole.

Haiku

新たにカットされたライトの列

a row of newly cut lights

新しい太陽から前に戻って

back in front from the new sun

smog en nombre del sol práctico

smog in behalf of the practical sun

atardecer tardío entre los girasoles marchitos

late sunset among the withered sunflowers

experiencia de las piedras que se utilizarán más adelante

experience of the stones that will be used later

en algunos casos el viento es simplemente el viento

in some cases the wind is plainly the wind

薄明かりをブラインドから一時的に保持する

holding twilight from a blind temporarily

震えた声の後に地面に

on the ground after a trembling voice

暗い通路の間で雷がまっすぐに伸びた

thunder straightened out among dark passages

Estado actual de suspenso de las luciérnagas apenas resuelto

present state of suspense of fireflies hardly settled

tarde o temprano una conspiración por cierto rayo

sooner or later a conspiracy by certain lightning

l'eau boueuse et perfide reste à moitié elle-même avant midi

treacherous muddy water remains half itself before noontide

新しい秋に次ぐ秋

new fall after fall

nouvel automne après automne

nueva caída tras caída

سقوط جديد بعد سقوط

ฤดูใบไม้ร่วงครั้งแล้วครั้งเล่า

bagong taglagas pagkatapos ng taglagas

一粒の沈黙の百倍

hundredfold of a grain of silence

影を減らすユリ

lily by its shadow reducing

herbe sauvage pensant probablement connaître ses formes

wild grass likely thinking knowing its forms

hierba silvestre probablemente pensando conociendo sus formas

la pluie presque des barres horizontales

the rain nearly horizonal bars

marcher sous des applaudissements lointains

marching with distant applause

distance left behind distance completed

Espero que sea una parte integral del despido.

hope an integral part of firing

لون النبيذ الأحمر يتنافس مع انعكاسه

colour of red wine competes with its reflection

สวนที่เต็มไปด้วยฝุ่นที่จะเติบโต

a garden full of dust to grow up

sa sandstorm sa sandstorm hindi masyadong malayo

in the sandstorm in the sandstorm not too far

sa bawat sulok ay isang eskultura ng buhangin

in every corner a sculpture of the sand

duststorm firmly established as windows

เด้งสูงอย่างเหลือเชื่อด้วยผลตอบแทนที่อ่อนแอ

bouncing impossibly high in a weak return

อากาศหน้าหนาวไม่เพียงแต่มีอยู่เท่านั้น

winter air becoming not only it exists

isang tiyak na asul ng pag-asa

a certain blue of expection

bukod sa sarili nito sa panahon ng pag-ulan ng stratosphere

aside from itself during rainstorm of stratrosphere

full space beyond names conceived

in the sermon on the mount bare feet ancher finally

บอระเพ็ดบานสองครั้งอย่างสงสัย

self-doubted wormwood blossoms twice

ลมเปียกไม่สั้นลงด้วยการเปลี่ยนแปลงที่อื่น

wet wind not shortened by a change elsewhere

sa pamamagitan ng pagbagsak ng mga bundok ng isang sheet ng sikat ng araw

through topple of mountains a sheet of sunlight

the stone's indifference remains with the flood

                              into the depths of Black Sea the place holy

women out there
crossing the rail
cross their shadows

candlelight around the shackles of the church

winter night and her fingerless fist on his pillow

snow falling—
the walls too white
to cover them

everywhere snow
and no windows
and no doors

beyond the horizon
and beyond the next horizon
deep sea

        ating mana ang tunog ng oras na ito

          our inheritance the sound of this hour

          expounding riddle with guitar and now

old pages roar and foam over

transparent rock
a line dividing
West and East

into the darkness
visibility
of the future

from light years
to candlelight length
we embrace cherries

the tallest waterfall
is thrice the length
of my father's shadow

a very long coconut tree
somewhere above
lies Africa

in Kisangani
in the morning dew
soldiers' blood on brush flowers

between my hands
a land of thicket
still not located

Stars fill my daughter's eyes.
In her sleeping
Giant four-o'clock blooms

to the north
direction of the grass
my hut also follows

the stars condense as tears at the funeral

heap of butterfly colours
build my hometown

tail of spring…
a wounded winter
still awake

my life story:
ghost at seaside
and smouldering wood

banana republic
beyond the Berlin wall
and morning clouds

collected smiles
a shade
for hungry children

a wind
turns a stone
then a gospel

My hometown
Is still sitting
On an old egg

She has come in
Very white in the darkness
This white lily

Inside the green bottle
A ruined state
And prosperous country

Among the ruins
I build my flight
And sunrise

Fleshpots of Egypt.
To bolt back,
Back is turned

In silent noise
In silent mind
In silent Tunisia

A bird has left
Its seed
In my future soil

My spring scatters
Water
In the public squares

Even in religiously
Divided household
Cherry still blossoms

The eyes of a tempestuous Welsh stallion ride
On the summer rainstorm
In DH Lawrence's grave

At the station, wild winds stare at
A desolate country.
Black purebred Arabian horses.

A mob of wild horses
Brave enough to tackle any weather
To cross even a joke

The swift October dusk
Tumbling among
The bruised potatoes

Something flying
From a swallow
To the Imperial Garden

A mariner explores Milky Way
With hurricane lamp
And our pains

A blink
Walking with Band Aid
Blue ribbon and bandit to heaven

Dante's rib cage
A mathematical formula
Someone suggests for the late rains

Positively charged sunflowers
Are eating up
Summer winds

Bending a rice farm
Bending a spring rain
Shape of the sky

winds of a butterfly
settles on the wet stone
and new dreams

an image
goes forth to conquer
its strength in the morning

under
a remembered bridge
full moon

something good
the heart of the dew
to be stirred soon

under a grain of sand
heavens roll
with mortal angles

a step
is trapped
in the edge
of autumn

the sun at midnight
the scepter of tomorrow
is guaranteed

first to be here
that will be the grass
next my body shell

around secant
desert storm
and lost tail

Congo mathematics
the sun's form
of notation

domain of a shadow
undefined
and leaves a gap

transparent Slovenia
a framed temple
on the rock

Ashanti doll:
the cliff melts
back to the sea

blazing sunlight
from the vault
Michelangelo's fresco

two rocks
crouching on each other
lives begin again

Ljubljana veal cutlet
and sunny beaches
the world as it was

Seven Years' War
territories blossom
over undefeated graves

Lipizzaner horse
more than 400 years
the sandstorm reappears

Istanbul midday
painting a cow
on the hill

leaving a single footprint
in the rhythm
of many feet

Rainbow
the difference
in exchange rates

noontide   first monthly payment

no passage
a boulder coming in
this morning

present too
is over to be
increased now

under
a remembered bridge
full moon

something good
the heart of the dew
to be stirred soon

(st

a

t)

ue

(o

f)

(de

w)

f
r
o
z
e
n

s
t
o
n
e
s

hanging   t o   the   end   o f   *used*   hope

                                        brig*H*t gre*N*ns in a brok*E*n gla*S*s

important

    port

            an

            ant

        or

import

a

WO man

and

i

are

waiting

with

statues

in

front

of

us

after

fall

we stop by our faith

distance **left** be**hind** my birth **reducing**

we

the winds

end in the wind

d *d* d d d d d d d

a a *a* a a a a a a a

w w *w* w w w w w

n n n *n* n n n n n n

f f f f f f f *f* f f f f

a a a a a *a* a a a a

l l l l l l l *l* l l l l l l

l l l l l *l* l l l l l l l

i i i i i i *i* i i i i i i i

n n n *n* n n n n n n

g g *g* g g g g g g g

i i i i i i i *i* i i i i i i i i

n n n n n *n* n n n n n

insects

   h i

   e l

   w e

   i n

   n c

   g e

blank

lank

ank

nk

k

p

u

r   f

m   e e t i n g

l   r

by   s

p u l s a t i o n

m   d   n   f   a

  y   i   e   a   g

       s   a   l   a

        t   r   l   i

      a   l   i   n

      n   y   n

       c   g

        e

aBc

tRiangle

eMerging

fRom

dEad

sHadows

too much in the next mirror i wait

thE

suN

iS

everY

thinG

afteR

dwaN

light distilling

                                    a day toward   august

into a kind of calm soft surprise

first

in

thirds

needing to flatten part of grit

next cold
a lizard
wetting
every
ground

the full casting of the sun

full casting of the sun

casting of the sun

ting of the sun

g of the sun

of the sun

f the sun

th sun

sun

on

  the

 sunward side

      of love making

a crab
walking sideway
cabbages in the sun

on the cliff
on the white clay
wet breeze below

thE

weiGht

  oF

  thE

horNs

aRe

  aLmost

  iN

   tOuch

a cloudless July day in that intimate area

at top of her voice we stand with morning

a train uses a bridge that connects the voices of my mothers details of your mind discolour the sea among cormorants

a smouldering world enters its third century

at the end of his wish this righting of the wrong

in your shadow i uproot forsythia plant

april sits on white eggs as casual employment unless dawn

a desire feeds on the sadness & suddenly sundown

a frozen mammoth
with grass in its mouth
after thousand years

in Palestine
a webbed feet-print
& 3 witnesses apply for it

everywhere I grow
immigrant, a nurse
& my wish emerge

already an hour
for house attendent to wake up
those in her dream

in the morning for the human spirit

a generous stone occupies the news

a few decades after rainfall saw dyslexia & my art

carefully looking at unfamiliar sand the wind wiats

from individuals to events to restore a dream i have seen

dewdrops
on the crystal vase
a face that astounds the wall

the strings of my guitar
are the streets
in Accra at noontide

the bridge
across the rainbow
bends toward my end

wild field of grammar
with no punctuation
& a small flower

the wet evening sun
an alien
with ice cubes

geometry country
only green hunts
only green sky

folding
its presence
among
the eyes left
beyond doubt
a white moth

lonely stars
missing
in the skull
& we are
convicted

a spring day
never-endng flat surface
framed by intersection

a piece of string
the same lenght
as the spring

the pain of a height street at dawn is transfered to me

behind the purple night
I chat with a crow
and the wounded grass

a big wheel running in the garden of pure wine making clouds

the price of rose petals in my dream is

a storm feeling powerless to help itself begins again

the sea of glass hides itself under a grain of stand

from here to the horizon is a tail of Leviathan

driving from rain to a day in my life

in the entrance

i have seen your image

but this time

in a sketch

hoping to paint one day

rooms inside you now are more spacious than Sundays

afterglw —

behind every smell

i shape

my nose

with your dance

        midnight

        after

        listening

        to your heart

yacht
in equation of moment
now as derivative

from equation of continuity
to uncertainty... clouds
elsewhere

 tangent to chamberlain's circle
chain of letters
from here to now

Eureka! his only shout
etymologist's tongue
painted like pale twilight

cerulean space
distance
of dy/dx

cot death among similar smiles

cotyledon
account of ten seconds
in the false ring

updated marriage   the total programme price

available draft   the shadow of the sun

instructional roads to the mandatory ages

the lungs of the dry ground unlimited skinning

april sky
the slate
half wet
half dry

rain falls
your heart

     still hardening

     rough draft—
butterfly shadows

       wetting the hamlet

wind
on winds

its shadows sweep

     distance away

morning smog -

   redheads about

  little *cinnamony candies*

in the crowdy weeds
a lily has stolen
the voice of the sandstorm

captured
in the whirlwind
the sand on another sand

cold air

    leans

   on

     stones

  sitting

   on

   each

    o

    ther

    ver

    ti

    ca

    l

    l

    y

sparrows fly   ~~~~~~~~~ over the s
                              u
                        n
                                   s e t
                                      i n g

^^^^^

^^^^^^^

^^^^^

on another
stepping stone

to begin again

            between boughs

spiderweb has trapped dew

          my next step

on barefooting

dawn like a door
opened to me

in the shop
natives buy the volcano
with red procession

in the dig

       a shadow

            lies below

                                          shadowofdewflowsbehind

in the dreamless place into the shapes of my forefathers

my

    grandmother

      mends

        cobwebs

          with

        a

        string

        of

        rain

        drops

BITINGGGGGGG
RAINNNNNNNN
WITHHHHHHHHH
SAMEEEEEEEEE
TEETHHHHHHHH
INNNNNNNNNN
THEEEEEEEEEE
BARKKKKKKKKK
OFFFFFFFFFFF
AAAAAAAAAA
TREEEEEEEEEEE

in my ribcage
a bird

nesting

winter

stillness

depends

too much

on winter

a
n   f
u   i
m   n
b   g
i   e
n   r
g   s
          h
          o
          l
          d
          i
          n
          g
          w
          e
          t
          w
          i
          n
          d
          s

| within |

| this |

| bonfire |

| the next day |

| will soon |

| spring |

| opening |

        a   n   w

        r   e   h

        i   a   e

        v   r   n

        e   a   r

        r   t   a

        c   r   i

        r   e   n

        o   e   s

        s   u   e

        s   n   m

        e   t   e

        s   i   r

        i   l   g

        t   f   e   s   r
        f

        r   i   r

        e   d   o

        f   a   m   l   y
        n

        e   o

        c   w

        t   h

        i   e

        o   r

        n   e

d=a=y=b=y=d=a=y=a=t=l=a=s=t=n=i=g=h=t

青い汚れは表面の下で青く染まります

blue

stains

blue

be

low

the

sur

face

not less

not more

   a strip

   of snow

be*neat*h me

un*ex*plored

the wind follows the willows

lighting the silence burning into grey

windless evening -
too many shadows
reappearing

behind night
is another night
behind night

under
a wing of butterfly
autumn sky

having
no house
no family
the housefly
leaves
a footprint
behind

now dark blue
now autumn
new autumn

Stormy autumn sea
Across to Turtle Mountains
Stretches the full moon

autumn gust -
the way hills travel
to themselves

November morning
hiding under
an exposed knife

cold at dawn
the wetness
penetrates
everything

deeper and deeper
i step
into the winter night

in the winter rain
i warm my body
to catch up

snowflake
i remember
the silent fly

in the genocide museum
snow
and snow

snowy field
how it stretches
from hands to hands

between apricot
and plangent colour
the blush at the heart

The size of the air
Just an hour ago
Among wet bodies

streetlights
and their flies
this is the way to go

morning clouds
and the time to wait
and cross

sun setting
yellow leaves
as tip off

new hedgerows
new bad debt
written off

among the sunflowers
I breathes myself
failing to breathe

two dancers look at each other
and agree through
the hollow gate

raindrop

collaps   ing

into it   self

without a   hint

of   noise

the apple tree
standing in the rain
how hard to see
through it

dewdrops
and thorns
around dewdrops

endless sunny beach
the bodies of rocks
are like their shadows

夜明け近くのカエデが枯れる

near dawn on maples withering

في مشهد من الخراب بعد الولادة

in a landscape of ruins after birth

clueless day

near by

the ruins

すぐに同人誌に光線を当てます

just a ray on a coterie shortly

ある程度になるまでワイヤーの端が結び目になり
ます

until it is num
the end of the wire
ends into a knot

antique watch
fobbing about -
sedate ceremony

measuring the depth
of a raindrop
I become the next raindrop

the rainclouds have gone
leaving their wetness
for the noon sun

staring right with distant eyes

painful silence grows around the grass

when a train
silently tugs away
from the station

full moonlit
unplugged and needing
a dusting

the forest floating
I am too old
to hold you firmly

gazing for a minute at the implausible icicle

正面から見て湿った空気を保持している

holding wet air in the front view

too weak to point
a pointer at the slithering
on the rock

opening the funeral and the rest of a day

a heart full of flowers
in the hills
I am the bee

at the ford
chimed footsteps run
into glare of memory

a low Victorian affair
in the drawing room -
black photographs

at snow-capped mountains
for sculptures
and pale white

stopping halfway
from watching the clover
I am rotting away

sitting on cemented bench
between statues
the passers-by look on

sun sparkling
all over the sand -
models exhibited

on lilies that grow in little leaps

a slate of rains leaning against uncompleted wall

hot desert expands on the bark of the wet winds where I start

a mountain pushes its height through the mist

the dandelions near the railway
are asking for
their new place

sparrows sleeping on the electric wire with no heads to count

heart of the distance
from my childhood
beating hard

empty

space

i

n

a

n

empty

space

re

mains

wet

af

ter

my

birth

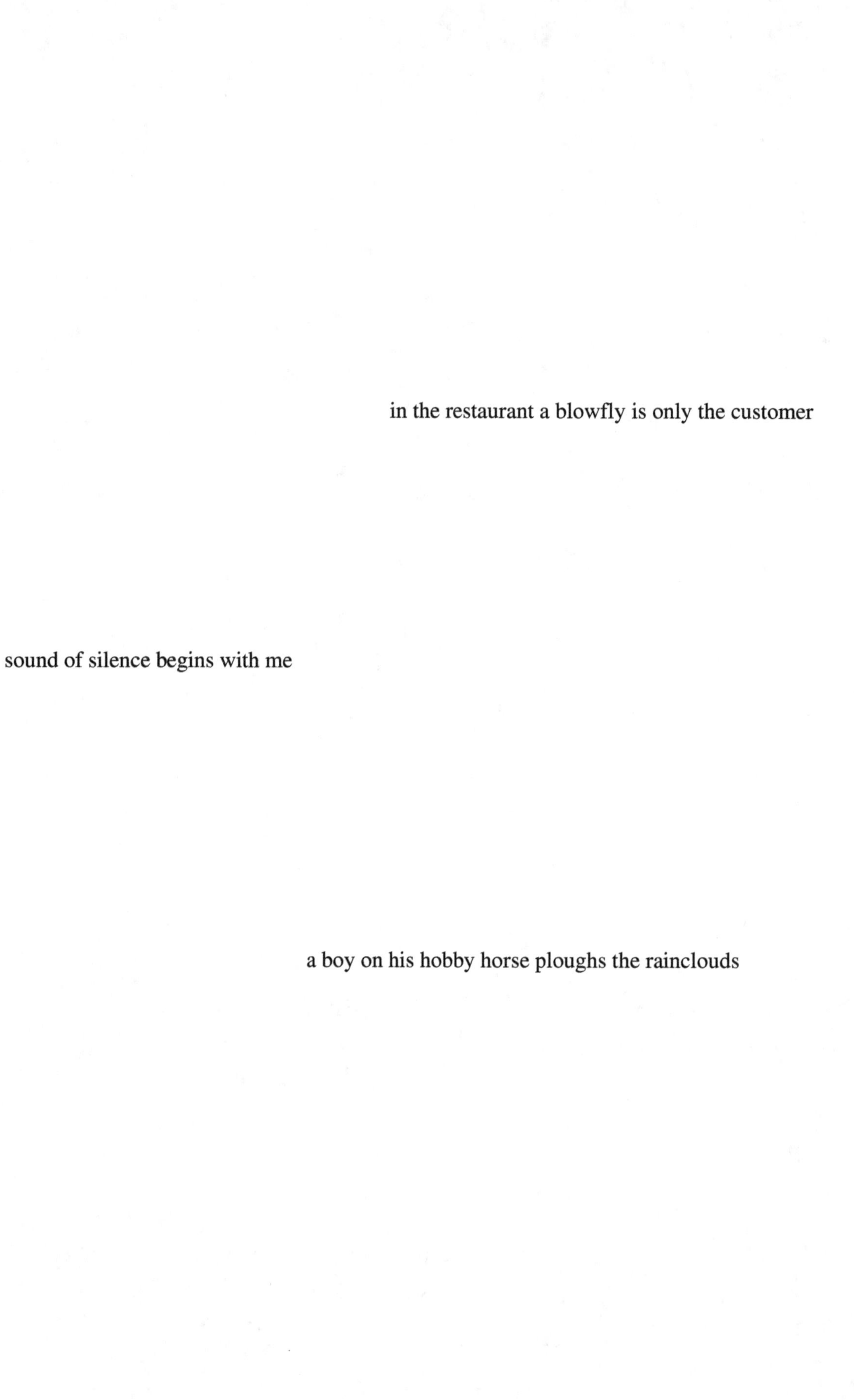

in the restaurant a blowfly is only the customer

sound of silence begins with me

a boy on his hobby horse ploughs the rainclouds

behind an echo i became winter

in a corner of the sandstorm
vodka and ghosts
seek for
a new empire

                                    shortly after my birth the new grass

placing night
by the flames
before days
are burned

in the north sky
i choose my first step
from here

a day is buried within monday

meanwhile the horizon
between *its* toes
the curd arching ford

by middle *state*
becoming the stand
plant *a rice field*

in the inner most heart
i begin my art & algebra
under the riot *shield*

after burnout to pursuit
career goals in ***the dig***
i reach near the top of my list

mist likely to fall down below

where ***many*** choose the colour
yeah, i ***need*** the income
& others ***around the same***

in severe pains among wounded stones

                                        i learn to spread like the hot breeze

explain to me
why the wood
is too hot this morning

my time just a night old

the night through the eyes of an owl fading away

a fragmental daybreak—
ashes and ashes
burning again

reopening a tomato suddenly duststorm

                              moonbathing and my tan cloth to cover a white cabbage

the smell of moonlight spreading across the public park

sudden dawn–
I remember where to hide
under a dragonfly's wing

in the midst of stars it is raining

in the south
a grain of sand
blocking every view

each individual
this grass stretches
from the burned ground

at the newspaper stand
rotten oranges
and special possession

a nude female statue watching a nude female statue

limping a remnant as far as to reside in the field

supporting group–
gajumaru trees scattered
with fellow travellers

the origin of indefinite the hollow within hollow

the hollow within hollow the origin of indefinite

of indefinite the hollow within hollow the origin

within the hollow the origin of indefinite hollow

the hollow the origin within hollow of indefinite

locking the next sandstorm behind the corpse

a thorny wood growing hair for the sunday market

around the lake somebody hiding the noontide

the crocuses are waiting for the crocuses behind

grass beyond telling direct dealings

in the shallow a shadow surfaces

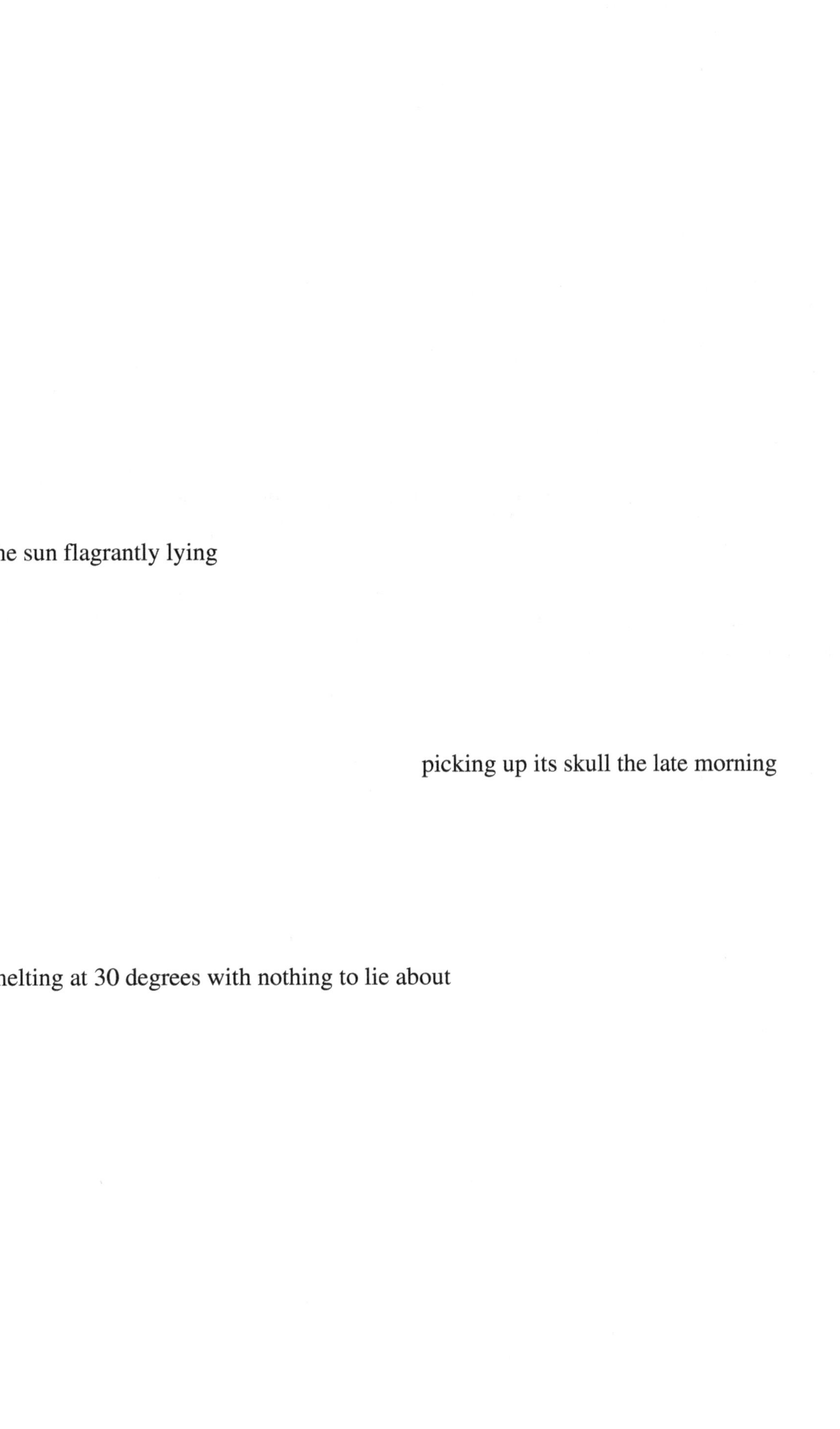

the sun flagrantly lying

picking up its skull the late morning

melting at 30 degrees with nothing to lie about

adhering to the thunder in my new posture

the man in the entrance
is evaporated milk
evaporating

between the eyes a dewy curtain

kangaroo hunter's hut a station following the night

along the avenue of roses fragrant of ruins

around the neck of a whisky bottle the signs to breathe

this garden

an archive

to host

the space

& status

reports

experts

instructors

have left

behind

automated

services

to walk through a hill-country
by lateral means
Varus again

on his ill-fated expedition another noontide

siege bank−
a continuous fence is erected
around increased numbers

with tea celebrants we end the pervious fall

everything is reduced
to wisps and hay and leather
in the hearth

on quietness of the first destruction

struggling with the hands around the morning smog

the blue pushing its hues through the noon clouds

a thin voice from the water in the voice fading

transparent country
upon a hill
attracting crows
from every direction

       dawn in hell

to stitch
someday
with

        an   ant

          perching on

           that temple

2 splits in clouds in the next clouds

           be hind bar bed wire   gyp so phi la & au gust sun

rib(cage
so cold)
with glass

[(#, #) = (*#)]

[(#, #) = (*#)], [(*, #) = ("#)]

[(#, #) = (*#)], [(*, #) = ("#)], [(", #) = (~ #)]

 [(A, a) = (Ba)]

place this with white lily
and another with red lily
somewhere to the north

eeeeeeeeeeeeeeerrrrrrrrrrrrrrrrrrrrr
rrrrrrrrrrrrrrrrrrrrreeeeeeeeeeeeeee
eeeeeeeeeeeeeeerrrrrrrrrrrrrrrrrrrrr
rrrrrrrrrrrrrrrrrrrrreeeeeeeeeeeeeee
eeeeeeeeeeeeeeerrrrrrrrrrrrrrrrrrrrr

the marble—
keeping an egg
from its fly

a ship emerging
from the mire—
this afterglow

the capital of a forest
rustling
remains in the distance

~~~~~~~~~~~~~~~~~~~~~~~~

~~~~~~~~~~~~~~~~~~~~~~~~

oooooooooooooooooo

~~~~~~~~~~~~~~~~~~~~~~~~

midnight
erasing the heads
in the head
~~~~~~~~~~~~~~~~~~~~~~~~

long bu*m*p *o*f t*on*gues too *lit*tle

白昼夢に近い深みに沈んでいく

sinking into a depth near daydreams

月曜日の入り口から平らにアクセス可能

a level access via the entrance to monday

r a y s

    b   m i   m
    u   y n   o
    i   o   a r
    l   l   y   n
    d   d   o   i
    i   a   u   n
    n   g t   g
    g   e h
                f
                u
                l

behind mirrors

   we appear

      in each other

squeezing sweat
from a stone
i remain the next statue

a long pathway half hydrangeas half a barmaid's call

windows
windows shut
windows shut within
windows shut within windows

whirlwind*performed*by*a*scythe

|c | |

|r |

|a | |

|c | |

|k | |

|s | |

| | |

| | |

|g | |

|l | |

|i | |

|s | |

|t | |

|e | |

|n | |

| i | |

|n | |

|g | |

| |

| | |

|r | |

|u | |

n	
n	
i	
n	
g

| | |

| |

|w |
|a |
|t |
|e |
|r |

*s * t * a * r * r * y **   n * i * g * h * t*

*** **** ******** ***** ***** *** **** ***

******* ****** ***** * * * * * * ******* * * *** * *

a dead geranium stands *   *   *   * near the shadows

space

  a b o v e

    s p a c e

    a b o v e

    s p a c e

teSday aPril nine

untied

sign(if)i(can)c.e.

con *ten* **ts** Of emp *tin* ess

cot(*Of*)*tage*

gecko licking clouds

acook

   acook

     o

     k

     s

in the afternoon into another tuft

whomeor   afterglow

the town of windmills of towns

+ + + + + + + + +

^ ^ ^^^ ^^ ^^ ^

- - - - - - - - - -

noonlit   field

t r e e s trees

        by accident

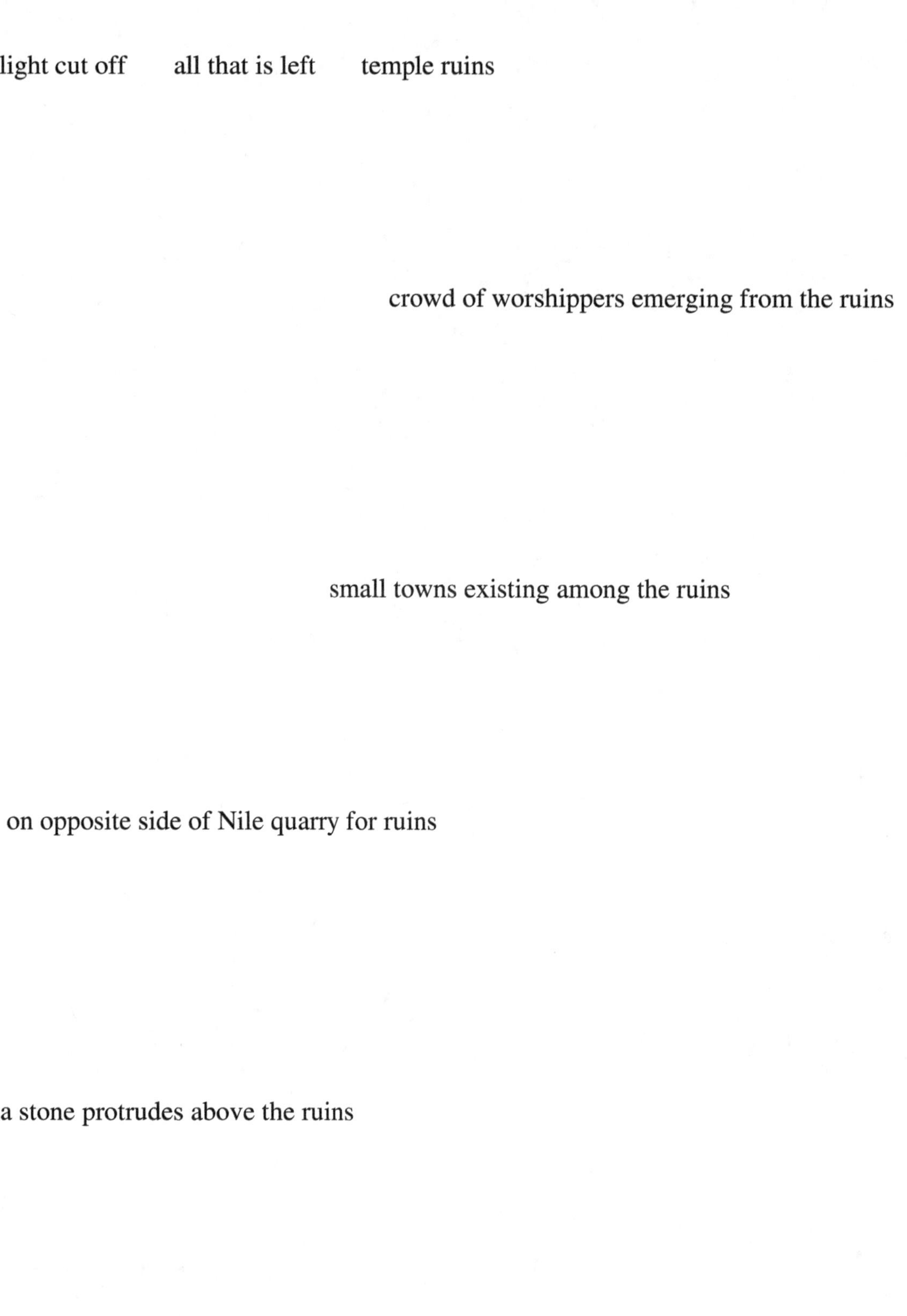
light cut off   all that is left   temple ruins

crowd of worshippers emerging from the ruins

small towns existing among the ruins

on opposite side of Nile quarry for ruins

a stone protrudes above the ruins

little remains except for their cemeteries

no   Egypt's once famous capital

                                                    the wall next behind the ruins

Arab conquerors flocking in Cairo   white sand

300 miles from Noph to Thebes   length of Nile

newspaper headlines in the infirmary

a small room

occupied by

emptiness

chairs

hardly noticed

by each other

full room

pain and morphine

floating across

still

holding up

the open window

a room

folded as

blank page

flood on flood
squatters' den
at Sodom and Gomorrah*

* Sodom and Gomorrah is a slum in Accra and perhaps the largest in Ghana.

digging through the fat on either margin

some names soft tyrannies around us to be named

anything

but this

or that

disapper

ing

in

the night

from

the gap

this

naming

skeletal shoreline staggered up from the endless naming

it is that weight
that holds me back
that name
that weight
behind the door

I want to be nameless
perhaps to be lighter
lighter than a dried leaf
falling with no sound

standing
inside
that small
cement cells

I squeeze
everything
from the stone
dawn

I seize
with your
false name
this haze

my limits
approaching
with direct
naming
in the rain

a window in black enough to be snow falling now

                                        this morning covers the distance built after a name

nam

ing

in

side

a

name

be

gins

to

glows

dim

 speaking
to myself
with the same kind of position

yes, griping nothing
after listening
to how to name your name
with thousand names

dust thrown out into the sea in someone's name

a path that grows after every shadow named after the sun

a set of names depict
silence-bound syntax
in a graveyard

what can I do
for the doors in the street
that runs after me

 to replace them
with names you peel
as oranges in the doors

on a footbridge
that separating
from your many parts

some names
chattering

under

some names
chattering

algún lugar tranquilo en algún lugar de México

someplace quiet down in Mexico somewhere

contents of a leaf falling emerge as negotiations

the enterprise so eagerly forwarded by whirlwinds

newspapers are frilled with floods by debunking artists

a feather falls within itself shortly

                                        thunder rolling into something else now

                              suddenly
                              a corner

                              in my life

                              thickly
                              overgrown

                              with grass

this foreign area
is a few days
after i left

                                        stillness has fallen on stillness for too long

        i am hosting the lost gull in my absence

rain
bubbles
reflect
themselves
in my thought

spring
to
spring
slow
ly

distance
e
dawn
r
s

drinking the sound of distant waterfall as long as i can

a star burning its way briefly

that wind like a butterfly spreading its wings

partially clouds form around a joint

deep silence falls in geometry

smoke rises from an illusion of future

afternoon mist behind the dilapidated walls

on the fence raindrops and their remains

in the wind longing for wind